ELEPHANT RESCUE

ELEPHANT RESCUE

Changing the Future for Endangered Wildlife

JODY MORGAN

FIREFLY BOOKS

A Firefly Book

Published by Firefly Books Ltd. 2004

First printing

PUBLISHER CATALOGING-IN-PUBLICATION DATA (U.S.)
Morgan, Jody.
Elephant rescue : changing the future for endangered wildlife / Jody Morgan.—1st ed.
[64] p. : col. photos. ; cm.
Includes index.
Summary: An exploration of elephants, their various habitats, the threat of extinction,
and the conservationists who are working with them.
ISBN 1-55297-595-9
ISBN 1-55297-594-0 (pbk.)
1. Elephants—Juvenile literature. 2. Wildlife conservation—Juvenile literature. (1. Elephants.) I. Title.
599.6/ 7 22   QL737.P98.M67   2004

NATIONAL LIBRARY OF CANADA CATALOGUING IN PUBLICATION DATA
Morgan, Jody
Elephant rescue : changing the future for endangered wildlife / Jody Morgan.
(Firefly animal rescue)
Includes index.
ISBN 1-55297-595-9 (bound).— ISBN 1-55297-594-0 (pbk.)
1. Elephants—Juvenile literature. 2. Endangered species—Juvenile
literature. I. Title. II. Series.
QL737.P98M67 2004   j599.67   c2003-906070-5

Published in the United States in 2004 by
Firefly Books (U.S.) Inc.
P.O. Box 1338, Ellicott Station
Buffalo, New York 14205

Published in Canada in 2004 by
Firefly Books Ltd.
66 Leek Crescent
Richmond Hill, Ontario, L4B 1H1

Design: Ingrid Paulson
Maps: Roberta Cooke

Printed in Singapore

*The Publisher acknowledges the financial support of the Government of Canada through the
Book Publishing Industry Development Program for its publishing activities.*

TABLE OF CONTENTS

THE GENTLE GIANT

"**I**f the tiger is the spirit of the jungle," says researcher Raman Sukumar, "the elephant is its body—large, majestic, making its presence felt with authority."

In some cultures, the elephant is treated as royalty or worshipped as a god. Yet through the centuries people have hunted them for their meat and ivory, harnessed them to pull logs out of the forest, even forced them to fight in wars. Growing human populations have destroyed most of the animal's territory and continue to compete for what's left.

Weighing up to 15,000 pounds (6,800 kg) and standing as tall as 13 feet (4 m), elephants are the largest of the land mammals. They are members of a group called Proboscidea, named for their most distinguishing feature: the proboscis, or trunk. Millions of years ago, over 350 species roamed every continent except Antarctica and Australia. The sole survivors are the African elephants (*Loxodonta africana* and *Loxodonta cyclotis*) and the Asian elephant (*Elephas maximus*). Strangely, their closest relative is the hyrax, a small, tailless mammal that looks like an overgrown guinea pig. They're also related to sea cows (manatees and dugongs) and aardvarks.

∧ An unlikely cousin: Slow-moving manatees are one among the elephant's closest living relatives.

In 1979, there were some 1.3 million elephants in Africa. By 1989, only 609,000 remained. That year, the world agreed to a total ban on the ivory trade, but the most recent tally suggests that their numbers have still not recovered, and may even be declining. The number of wild Asian elephants has also dropped dramatically in the past 50 years; only 36,000 to 44,000 remain in the wild.

Today, devoted conservationists and scientists are working to find new ways for people and elephants to live together.

7

WHAT BIG BRAINS YOU HAVE

It's not just the elephant's size that inspires awe and wonder. Its intelligence and personality, its elaborate social life, the way it cares for its young and grieves for its dead, its sophisticated communication—all of these qualities set elephants apart from other animals.

∧ The elephant-headed Hindu deity Ganesh is worshiped as the god of wisdom, remover of obstacles and bringer of good fortune.

An animal's intelligence is related to brain size, and at between 9 and 13 pounds (4 to 6 kg), an elephant's brain is the biggest among land animals'. Like those of humans, apes and dolphins, elephant brains are also extremely complex—this, too, is a measure of intelligence. It's often said that elephants never forget, and with good reason. The area of the brain that handles memory is so large in an elephant that it bulges out at the sides.

In Asia, young working elephants learned to stuff the wooden bells around their necks with mud to stop them from ringing. They could then steal silently into farmers' fields at night to take bananas. Elephants have been known to hold tree branches in their trunks in order to scratch hard-to-reach spots or remove parasites. Matriarchs, the lead females in social groups, can remember and guide their families to prime feeding areas and watering holes—even if years have passed since their last visit.

Like humans, elephants care for one another. The matriarch, in particular, will put herself at risk, facing down poachers while the rest of her family escapes. Elephants may gather around a wounded comrade to offer support. After a death, surviving members often stand by for days in a clear display of grief. Likewise, they will cover their dead with branches, leaves and grass, as if burying them. When they come across elephant bones, they sniff and stroke them with their trunks, and may even pull out the tusks to shatter them against a tree or rock.

Like humans, elephants care for one another. Here, family members stand watch over a > tranquilized elephant.

WHERE DO ELEPHANTS LIVE?

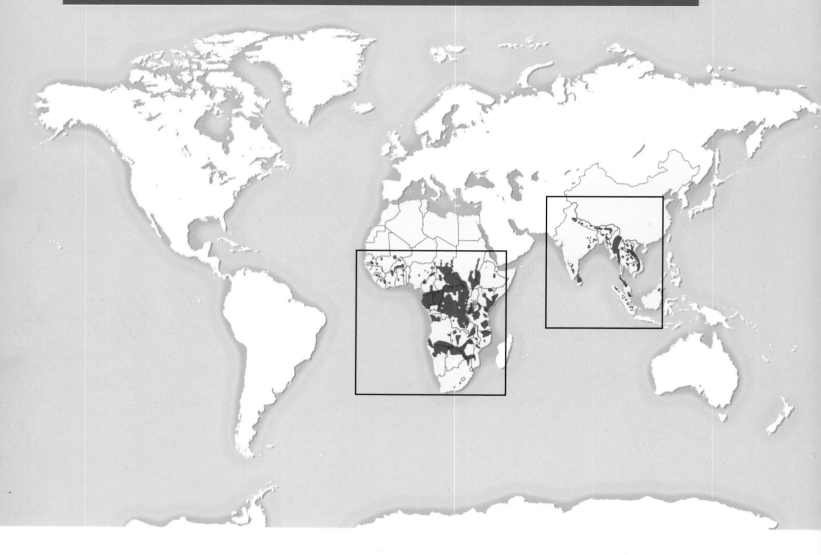

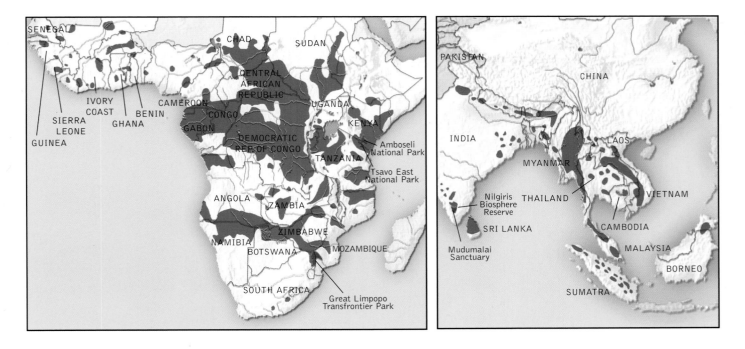

Of the three elephant species, we're most familiar with the savanna, or bush elephant (*Loxodonta africana*), which lives on Africa's plains. But about one-third of that continent's elephants live in dark, dense, often inaccessible rainforests. These are the African forest elephants, *Loxodonta cyclotis*, which are distinctly smaller than their savanna cousins. Their ears are smaller and more rounded, and their tusks, which point downward, are straighter and more slender. Their highly prized ivory has a slight pinkish tint.

Small populations of Asian elephants are found in 13 countries and have been divided into three subspecies. *Elephas maximus indicus* is found in India and Southeast Asia, *Elephas maximus maximus* inhabits Sri Lanka, and *Elephas maximus sumatranus* lives on the Indonesian island of Sumatra.

THE STORY SO FAR

With a population only one-tenth that of their African relatives, Asian elephants are at greatest risk. Their biggest threat is habitat destruction. Many are also illegally captured for domestic use, and they are killed for their tusks and meat.

In Africa, the most immediate danger is poaching for ivory. Since 1989, when the international trade in ivory was banned, the continent's elephant population has showed some signs of recovery. But the ban has twice been temporarily lifted to allow some countries to sell off stored ivory. This practice, conservationists caution, can lead to a resurgence in poaching.

∧ A game warden with the Kenyan Wildlife Service sorts through a seizure of illegal ivory.

1972 Cynthia Moss starts the Amboseli Elephant Research Project, now the world's longest-running study of wild elephants.

1975 The Convention on International Trade in Endangered Species (CITES) comes into force. The Asian elephant is immediately placed on Appendix I: all trade in its parts is declared illegal.

1979 Biologists estimate there are 1.3 million elephants in Africa. A decade later, the number has been halved, primarily due to poaching, with up to 300 elephants killed daily.

1989 President Daniel arap Moi of Kenya torches the ivory of about 2,000 poached elephants—worth over $3 million (U.S.)—to draw attention to the plight of elephants and support the ban on the ivory trade. Three months later, CITES announces it will grant African elephants the highest level of protection.

1990 The CITES ban on trading African elephant ivory comes into effect, and the market collapses. Poaching declines by up to 90 percent.

1991 Project Elephant is launched in India, to ensure the long-term survival of Asian elephants and reduce human-elephant conflict.

1995 Conservation groups in India initiate a new project to monitor poaching and determine the effect of the illegal ivory trade on wild populations.

In 1989, the Kenyan government set fire to over $3 million (U.S.) worth of poached ivory to signal its commitment to a worldwide ivory-trade ban.

1997 Three African countries lobby for a one-time sell-off of legally acquired raw ivory to Japan. CITES agrees to the sale on the condition that new monitoring systems are established to track poachers.

1999 The sale of 55 tons (50,000 kg) of ivory goes ahead. Some conservationists argue that not all of the CITES conditions were fulfilled.

2000 CITES votes to continue enforcing the total ivory ban.

2002 The biggest haul of illegal ivory since 1989—equivalent to the tusks of more than 600 elephants—is seized in Singapore.

2003 The Kenyan Wildlife Service seizes 33 tusks—its biggest ivory seizure in three years. Poachers, dealers and traders take it as a signal that the ivory trade is about to reopen.

TUSK TUSK

Humans have long prized the ivory from elephant tusks. It is carved into figurines, ornaments, jewelry and other decorative items.

Tusks are giant incisor teeth that continue to grow throughout the elephant's lifetime. Most male Asian elephants have tusks, but tuskless males, known as *makhnas* in India, are also common. In Asian females, the tusks are called tushes, and are too small to be seen or absent altogether. Both male and female African elephants have tusks, although the male's are much larger, heavier and faster growing. The record length for an African male tusk is over 11 feet (3.4 m)—much taller than a basketball hoop—and the heaviest weighed a stunning 259 pounds (118 kg). It's no wonder that older males are prime targets for ivory hunters.

∧ Asian female elephants either are tuskless or have very small tusks called tushes. Male tusks are usually more visible, but some males have no tusks.

Elephant calves are born with a set of "milk tusks" that fall out and are replaced with permanent tusks when the calf is 6 to 12 months old. As the tusks grow, they become an invaluable tool. The sharp ends are helpful in digging for water, salt and roots, and prying bark from trees. Domestic elephants in Asia use their tusks as forklifts to carry logs. Males, especially, use them as weapons when defending mates or to display superiority. Tusks can even serve as a resting place for a tired 300-pound (135 kg) trunk.

Just as a person is left- or right-handed, an elephant tends to favor one tusk over the other. The preferred tusk develops a blunter tip, with more cracks and scars. Differences in tusk size, shape and direction help scientists to identify individual elephants.

< Tusks, giant incisor teeth that grow about 7 inches per year, are handy tools for prying bark off trees.

WHITE GOLD

Herds of elephants in North Africa were hunted to extinction for their ivory long before Europeans arrived in the 18th and 19th centuries. But when Europeans and Americans raised the demand for this "white gold" in jewelry, sculptures, piano keys and even billiard balls, the elephants in southern and western Africa also began to disappear.

∧ This body of an elephant, poached only for its valuable tusks, has been left to rot.

In 1894, South Africa created the Pongola Reserve, the world's first wildlife sanctuary. And when more laws to protect elephants were introduced in the early 20th century, many populations began to recover. With the invention of plastics and a drop in the price of ivory following the First World War, the demand for ivory plummeted.

But when major ivory-carving centers like Japan devised new uses for ivory in the 1970s and 1980s, demand again skyrocketed. By the mid-1980s, 300 elephants were being killed each day, and an overwhelming 80 percent of the tusks in the trade came from poached elephants.

The Convention on International Trade in Endangered Species (CITES) finally announced a worldwide ban on the trade of ivory, which came into effect in January 1990. The ivory market quickly collapsed and poaching nosedived. In July 1997, however, Zimbabwe, Botswana and Namibia convinced CITES to approve a one-time sale of stockpiled ivory to Japan, on the condition that the countries set up monitoring systems to track poachers and measure the effect of the ivory trade on elephant populations. Despite protests from conservationists and scientists, the sale went ahead in April 1999.

Some African countries want to sell stockpiled ivory to help fund their environmental programs.

In April 2000, CITES voted to continue the ban, but in November 2002 it agreed to let Namibia, Botswana and South Africa sell about 66 tons (60,000 kg) of stockpiled ivory, collected from elephants that had died naturally. The sale will take place after May 2004, if the three countries meet certain conditions, including monitoring populations and passing laws to control any illegal trade.

Conservationists are concerned that these decisions send a message to poachers that the ivory trade has resumed, and that a new round of slaughter will begin.

THE HIGH COST OF POACHING

Poaching has taken a great toll on the African elephant. There are few males left more than 40 years old—most have been slaughtered for their ivory. Since tusk size is an inherited characteristic, taking the animals with the largest tusks out of the breeding pool reduces the average tusk size in later generations. It is now rare to find a tusk weighing over a hundred pounds.

As older, larger and healthier elephants are killed, poachers turn their weapons on younger elephants; they must kill many more of these to get the desired amount of ivory. These hunters are ridding populations of their healthiest genetic material.

By killing off matriarchs, poachers are also wiping out the herd's "memory," without which it is more difficult for them to find traditional sources of food and water, raise their calves and defend themselves.

HERD MENTALITY

African savanna elephants live in tightly knit family groups of related females, or cows, and their offspring. A family may have as few as six members, or as many as 20. Asian elephants live in smaller groups of up to 11 females. Forest elephants live in groups of only two or three, perhaps because they encounter fewer predators.

Families are led by the oldest and most experienced female, known as the matriarch. Over the course of her life, some 40 to 50 years, the matriarch gathers a wealth of knowledge about the family's home range, migratory routes, the best feeding spots and how to avoid threats. The family relies on her to make important decisions. When a matriarch is killed—a common occurrence, since she usually has the largest tusks in the group—the others are more vulnerable to drought and enemies.

When families meet after a long separation, they erupt in excitement.

The family's bonds are strong, and females of all ages pitch in to care for the calves. Females stay with their families for life, even once they have their own babies. Males, or bulls, however, leave when they reach about 14 years old. They sometimes head off to live with groups of bachelor bulls of different ages, or they simply go it alone.

If a family grows too large or is threatened by food shortages, some members leave and form their own families. Yet they maintain close contact with the original family for life. When these related families, or bond groups, meet after being separated for a while, they erupt in excitement: waving ears, entwining trunks, rumbling, clicking tusks and twirling in circles.

Clans are collections of bond groups that share the same home range but are not necessarily related. Right after the rainy season, when the land is lush with food, clan members come together in congregations of up to a thousand animals.

19

Iain Douglas-Hamilton arrived at Lake Manyara National Park in Tanzania in 1965. He set up camp under a tree beside the sparkling Ndala River, tucked beneath the high cliffs of the Rift Valley. The young Scottish scientist had set out to identify each elephant in the area with the help of a young Tanzanian park ranger. Wandering through thick vegetation, the pair collected clues and samples and snapped pictures to help them in their quest.

∧ Iain Douglas-Hamilton conducted the first aerial surveys of Africa's elephants, and continues to fight for their survival.

Douglas-Hamilton met his future wife and partner, Oria, in 1969. Together they continued the study of wild elephants in Manyara, launching a groundbreaking project that used radio collars to track the animals' movements. The couple even raised their two daughters, Saba and Dudu, among the elephants. A young female known as Virgo was especially comfortable around the family: Douglas-Hamilton could safely hold his daughter only inches away from Virgo's raised trunk.

After a two-year stay in England, the family returned to Manyara in 1973 and were appalled to hear about the elephant slaughter that had occurred as the price of ivory soared. At that point, Douglas-Hamilton recalls, they dedicated their lives to creating a future for the elephants. "It was a battle which would be fought on the field and in the conference rooms," he writes in his book *Battle for the Elephants*. "We would join those involved in a never-ending battle for money to pay for run-down national parks and raggle-taggle anti-poaching forces. The battle would be fought from the skies and on the ground, shooting and getting shot at in bloody skirmishes with heavily armed poachers."

Save the Elephants includes local people in research and conservation projects, and works to foster positive attitudes toward elephants in African communities.

The public needed to be convinced of the animal's plight. From their small airplane, the couple made the first surveys of African elephants. They gathered solid statistics, showing how elephant populations and habitats were changing.

In 1993, the couple founded Save the Elephants, a charity that supports a variety of research projects, including many that use radio collars to track long-distance movements. It also strives to help African communities develop positive attitudes toward elephants, through public education and local involvement.

They've been at it more than three decades, but for the Douglas-Hamiltons, the fight for the African elephant continues.

∧ A dazed elephant struggles to its feet after being shot with a dart. The tranquilizer enables researchers to fit the animal with a radio collar.

Years ago, hunters paid tens of thousands of dollars for the chance to shoot and kill a bull elephant in South Africa's Timbavati Private Nature Reserve. Today, they pay the same amount to shoot and tranquilize the animal with a dart. The elephant suffers no harm, researchers can fit the elephant with a radio collar and money is brought in for conservation.

Iain Douglas-Hamilton came up with the idea of "green hunting" as an alternative to lethal sport-hunting. It's a win-win situation, as he explains. "For those who find an elephant too intelligent to shoot for sport, here you can have a sporting hunt without an ethical downside, while helping conserve the species."

Once a tranquilized bull goes down, the hunter and a team of experts quickly measure the sleeping animal and fit it with a radio collar. The bull can then be tracked by satellite, which provides crucial information for managing the species. Then everyone retreats while a wildlife veterinarian injects an antidote, and within minutes, the elephant is back on its feet.

The hunter poses for a photograph with the sleeping elephant and is presented with a plaster trophy made from a cast of its tusks. Every six months, the hunter receives information about his elephant's whereabouts.

Green hunting provides crucial information for managing elephants.

Since the first time in November 1998, five elephants have been green-hunted. Each is a living trophy that shows how creative thinking can help conserve a magnificent species.

When Cynthia Moss traveled to Africa as a journalist in 1967, it was a trip that would change her life. "Within a week, I had this overwhelming sense that I'd come home," she remembers.

∧ In Amboseli National Park, Cynthia Moss (**LEFT**) and her research assistants use a radio tracking device to glean information about elephants.

Moss returned to Africa five months later to work as an elephant researcher's assistant in Tanzania, although she had had no formal scientific training. In 1972 she launched her own study, the Amboseli Elephant Research Project (AERP), at Amboseli National Park in Kenya.

The park was an ideal site for studying elephants—150 square miles (240 km²) relatively untroubled by humans. Its small elephant population had not been heavily poached, and lived much as it had for generations. Since her arrival, Moss has identified and named more than 1,800 elephants and witnessed the daily dramas of births, battles, play, death and survival, almost as though she were a family member.

Now more than 30 years old, AERP is the longest-running study of wild African elephants, and its research has contributed significantly to elephant conservation and welfare. "Our work in Amboseli has changed people's attitudes towards elephants, particularly in regard to our treatment of them both in the wild and in captivity," Moss says proudly. "Our studies have made people think of ethical considerations regarding elephants."

Moss continues to dedicate her life to the survival and well-being of Africa's elephants. She teaches elephant observation to African scientists and wildlife personnel, and has initiated programs to help elephants and humans share the land peacefully.

Elephants amble across the open plains of Amboseli National Park, home of the world's longest-running study of big land animals, the Amboseli Elephant Research Project.

She has also written passionately about her work: "My priority, my love, my life are the Amboseli elephants, but I also want to ensure that there are elephants in other places that are able to exist in all the complexity and joy which elephants are capable of. It may be a lot to ask, but I think it is a goal worth striving for."

AT WORK | JOYCE POOLE

Kenya native Joyce Poole knew from the age of 11 that she wanted to study elephants. After studying zoology at an American college, the 19-year-old Poole arrived in Amboseli National Park in 1975 to join Cynthia Moss's already prestigious elephant study. It was both a joyful homecoming and the beginning of a life-long passion.

∧ An impressive and threatening display by a charging bull elephant.

Poole began studying bull elephants, and eventually became acquainted with more than 800 individuals of both sexes, from the playful Joshua to the terrifying Bad Bull, who threatened her when she came too close and once chased her across the plains. Poole followed the elephants in Amboseli closely, learning about their family life and social structure. "Watching elephants with their bones leaves me with little doubt that they have an understanding of their own mortality, that they have a sense of self," she says. "And is it so hard to imagine that an animal that lives for 60 or 70 years in a tight-knit social group has an understanding of time, a concept of past and future?"

Poole has made important discoveries about male elephant sexual cycles. She determined that African male elephants, like their Asian cousins, experience "musth," a period of heightened aggression and eagerness to mate. She also pioneered work on communication by recording and analyzing elephant calls with highly sensitive equipment. She was part of the research team that revealed that elephants appear to have their own language. So far, Poole has identified 75 different vocalizations. She and her husband, Petter Granli, have since launched the Savanna Elephant Vocalization Project, an attempt to analyze the entire sound repertoire of savanna elephants.

Joyce Poole patiently observes a mother and her calf. She has spent almost three decades studying elephant behavior and social structure.

The terrible slaughter of Kenya's elephants in the mid-1980s convinced Poole to invest her energy in ending the ivory trade. With many of her fellow researchers, she played a part in securing the 1989 ivory ban, and in 1990 Poole was appointed Director of the Kenya Wildlife Service Elephant Programme.

Almost three decades after returning to Kenya, Poole made another homecoming of sorts: she returned to the Amboseli project. In her new role as scientific director she oversees data collection, works with visiting scientists and initiates new research. Poole also continues to carry out her own work with the elephants she knows and loves—research that's vital in planning effective programs for their survival.

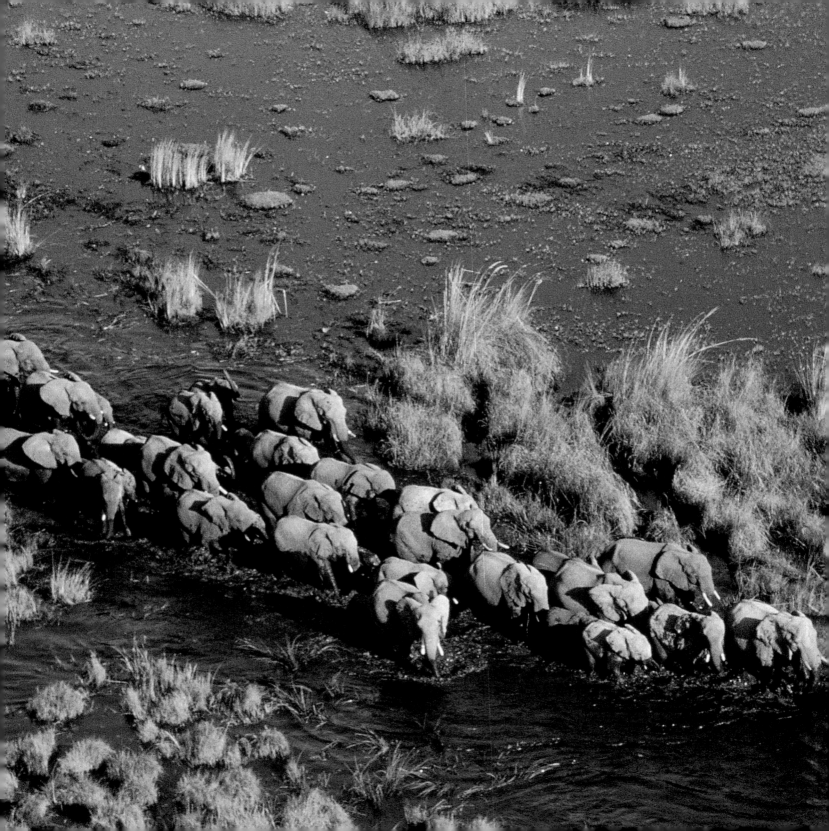

HAVE TRUNK, WILL TRAVEL

We often think of elephants as living on savannas surrounded by lions, giraffes and zebras, but Africa's elephants live in a variety of habitats. One third to one half dwell in the continent's dark, dense, hard-to-reach rainforests. A rare population even thrives in the desert of Namibia, in southern Africa. Able to go for days without water, these desert elephants display a remarkable ability to remember the location of a water hole, even if they haven't visited the site for months.

Asian elephants prefer the shady environment provided by forests. But with exploding human populations, many forests have been cleared for farming or timber. Conservationists predict the Asian elephant will have little future outside parks and protected reserves.

In order to find enough of the hundreds of plants on their menu, elephants need to roam a great deal of land. A typical home range for African elephants is 200 to 400 square miles (320 to 640 km²), but can be as large as 1,200 square miles (1,900 km²). During dry seasons, they may travel up to 30 miles (50 km) a day in search of food and water. Asian elephants wander over smaller areas of 65 to 190 square miles (100 to 300 km²).

Triggered by the cycle of wet and dry seasons, they also make long journeys in search of food and water, traveling 3,000 to 6,000 miles (4,800 to 9,700 km) in twelve months. Year after year, the elephants follow these same routes. But as human populations grow, traditional migration routes shrink or are destroyed. Multiplying farms, roads and villages restrict elephant herds to protected areas in national parks.

Conservationists are working hard to fight this trend. In India, for example, special corridors—connecting bands of suitable habitat—have been set up to allow the elephants to move between protected areas. By 2050, Africa's population will more than double, and Asia's will increase by almost half. Even if conservationists manage to control the ivory crisis, shrinking and altered habitats caused by booming human populations pose the single biggest threat to the elephant's long-term survival.

TRAMPLED UNDERFOOT

Humans and elephants both need land with sufficient food and water, and finding enough to go around is a challenge. As their populations overlap, they must compete for the same scarce resources. Farmers across Asia and Africa lose millions of dollars each year when elephants raid their fields and eat or trample their crops. Both farmers and elephants have lost their lives in the struggle.

Conservationists, scientists and farmers are trying to find ways to reduce the conflict. Many farmers receive government funds to help pay for crop damage. Some have tried digging concrete-lined trenches around farms, and installing electric fences, to discourage elephants from entering. But trenches are expensive to dig and maintain, and they fill with water during heavy rain. Elephants have even learned to cross trenches by digging up the soil. Fences are also costly, and male elephants can use their tusks to break the wire. Other elephants push trees on top of the fences.

Both farmers and elephants have died in the struggle.

Zoologists have come up with a pepper-spray bomb that combines chili pepper and oil, which burn the inside of elephants' sensitive noses. It seems to be doing the trick. Sprayed elephants leave fields in a hurry, suffering no permanent damage; and the memory of the spray discourages them from returning. Many farmers in Zimbabwe have begun planting fields of chili peppers. Burning some of these peppers keeps the elephants away from their crops, and the remaining chilies are sold in markets.

In Thailand, some fruit growers have given up the fight to protect their crops, and are switching to dairy farming in hopes of living peacefully alongside the elephants.

When too many elephants live in a confined area, they can destroy entire ecosystems by stripping vegetation, knocking down trees, and posing a risk to wildlife and humans. One short-term solution is relocation to areas with fewer people. This is costly and sometimes dangerous, but it has been done successfully in Kenya, where 30 elephants were moved from Mwaluganje Elephant Sanctuary, a unique forest they were destroying, to Tsavo East National Park.

When the gate between South Africa and Mozambique was opened in a ceremony on October 4, 2001, the world witnessed the start of one of the biggest mass relocations of elephants ever attempted. Through the gate passed 40 elephants, the first of 1,000 scheduled to be removed to Mozambique over three years.

> ## If all goes according to plan, elephants and other wildlife will once again roam their traditional migration routes.

Moved in family groups, the elephants were first tranquilized and measured. Once blood samples were taken and diseases ruled out, they were given antibiotics and loaded onto trucks by a mobile crane. They were driven, still sleeping, across the border to an enclosed area, where they had a few days to adapt to their new surroundings. Some were radio-collared so that their movements could be monitored.

Elephant relocation is just the first step in the creation of a new "peace park" that will change the face of conservation in Africa. The Great Limpopo Transfrontier Park links South Africa, Mozambique and Zimbabwe and covers a stretch of land only slightly smaller than Switzerland. Some experts predict it will host an unprecedented range of plants and animals.

The park is the first phase in a master plan that will serve both animals and people. Other international parks in southern Africa are in the works. The movement is led by The Peace Parks Foundation, the brainchild of the World Conservation Union and World Wildlife Fund—and politicians who see the benefit of pulling down fences that divide not only countries, but entire ecosystems. If all goes according to plan, elephants and other wildlife will once again roam their traditional migration routes. Healthier breeding populations should become established, and the animals will be protected by specially trained rangers and staff. Tourists, too, will travel freely across international borders, creating jobs and boosting local economies.

Former South African president Nelson Mandela opens the South African border to allow a group of elephants to cross into Mozambique. The elephants are the first to be relocated into a new cross-border game park that will change the face of African conservation.

The Great Limpopo Transfrontier Park was christened by the leaders of the three countries in a fence-cutting ceremony in December 2002. But officials will consider the park truly established only when there is totally free movement of animals and people in Africa. The Peace Parks Foundation's vision is "an Africa where the elephant roams and the roar of the lion shatters the night, where people can reap the benefits of nature and in turn support her."

YOU ARE WHAT YOU EAT

Each day, a full-grown elephant eats between 200 and 900 pounds (90 to 410 kg) of food, and drinks up to 50 gallons (190 l) of water. Feeding usually takes place in spurts throughout the morning, afternoon and night.

An elephant is a herbivore, devouring only plants from the root to the fruit. In some areas, elephants may eat 200 different species. The bulk of the African savanna elephant's diet is grass, but fruit is a favorite treat when available. During the dry season, when the grass is withered, elephants turn to bark and rough vegetation, such as the branches of the acacia tree, with its 2-inch (5 cm) needle-sharp thorns. The forest elephant dines heavily on fruit as well as leaves, twigs and bark.

If an elephant needs more salt in its diet, it will break off chunks of salty rock or soil with its tusks, then lob them into its mouth with its trunk. A salt-hungry elephant may eat up to 50 pounds (23 kg) of saline soil in an hour.

An elephant skillfully harvests food with its tusks, trunk and feet. Propped up on its hind legs the animal can use its trunk to pluck fruit and leaves from a tree more than 30 feet (9 m) tall. Elephants also use their trunks to pull entire plants out of the ground and strip them of leaves. They clean freshly harvested plants by beating them against their legs, while tusks can peel nutritious bark off trees.

∧ Elephants can go for up to four days without water, and when water sources dry up, the elephant uses its tusks to dig wells.

< Elephants eat an incredible range of vegetation and spend about 16 hours a day foraging and feeding.

MAKE YOURSELF AT HOME

Whether they live in a savanna, woodland or desert, elephants are one of the few species that are capable of transforming their habitat. This makes them a "keystone species." In fact, many scientists consider elephants a "super keystone species," since the changes they make can actually benefit other animals.

By going about their daily lives, elephants act as landscape architects. Pulling twigs and branches off trees and bushes, they effectively prune the vegetation, causing it to grow back thicker than before. As they knock over trees in the forest, sun-loving plants take over, transforming the woodland into grassland and providing new homes for dozens of other species.

∧ Undigested plant material in elephant dung is a food source for invertebrates.

Even elephant dung plays a crucial role. As an elephant moves around its habitat, dropping up to 200 pounds (90 kg) of dung a day, it spreads plant seeds. These quickly germinate and eventually grow into new food sources.

Elephants also provide food for other herbivores by knocking down branches, twigs, fruit and leaves that smaller creatures couldn't otherwise reach. Birds depend on the insects and reptiles that are stirred up when elephants sway through grass. Generations of elephants digging for underground salt in Mount Elgon, Kenya, has resulted in huge caves that provide homes for bats, monkeys and other animals.

Following the same paths day after day, particularly in forests, elephants construct "highways" for other animals—including humans. These paths function as fire breaks, too, and as channels for rain runoff.

In uprooting trees and stripping off bark and vegetation, elephants are effectively > changing their habitat—often to the benefit of other animals.

As his plane circles above the thick bush in Samburu, Kenya, Iain Douglas-Hamilton is on the lookout for a tall, distinguished matriarch known as Goya. On the ground are two support vehicles and a team of Save the Elephants researchers, rangers and veterinarians. They are poised to outfit the 6,000-pound (2,700 kg) elephant with an extra large, 13-pound (6 kg) radio collar—not an easy task.

∧ Iain Douglas-Hamilton checks the position of an elephant wearing a Global Positioning System (GPS) beacon, in Meru National Park, Kenya.

Once Douglas-Hamilton's radio detects Goya's precise location, the team's job is to tranquilize her. Hidden behind a curtain of brush, Goya is an elusive target. Even after the team gets off a perfect shot, the huge animal lumbers out of sight once more. Within four minutes, however, Douglas-Hamilton locates the sleeping elephant and the team moves in. With Goya's family watching intently from just a hundred feet (30 m) away, team members fit her with a collar. Others collect hair, blood and skin samples. Once she has been measured, she is injected with an antidote to the tranquilizer. This quickly takes effect, and a dazed Goya staggers to her feet and rumbles a message that brings the family running to her side. The reunited group slips away unharmed. The process has taken all of 10 minutes.

Iain Douglas-Hamilton has been radio-collaring elephants since the 1960s. More recently, he and his colleagues have pioneered a Global Positioning System (GPS) elephant tracking technique, which uses satellites to follow the animals' movements continuously. The sophisticated GPS collars must stand up to serious abuse: extreme pressure, heat and cold, and daily immersion in water.

Dwarfed by a tranquilized elephant, Iain Douglas-Hamilton fits it with a radio collar.

Each collar is equipped with a grab bag of electronics, including sensors that collect and store data about elephant activity levels, motion and location. When the data is downloaded and analyzed, it reveals vital information about home ranges, movement in relation to predators, and availability of food and water. "By using GPS and other technologies to monitor and track the elephants' movements," says Douglas-Hamilton, "we have been better able to understand the elephant's needs and attain our ultimate goal of helping save them and their habitat."

Armed only with flashlights and a notebook, elephant researcher Raman Sukumar and his assistant slog through grain fields near the village of Hasanur in southern India. Eventually they reach the treetop platform where they will spend the night, on the lookout for crop-raiding Asian elephants.

Suddenly their lights detect a single radiant-white tusk in the darkness. Sukumar instantly recognizes Vinay, a large bull whose right tusk has broken off. The notorious crop raider has come to the fields at least 120 nights in the past year. Despite farmers' efforts to chase him away, Vinay spends the night calmly pulling out chunks of shoots. At dawn, after having downed a quarter-ton of ragi, a staple grain in this region, the satisfied elephant lumbers off to the jungle to catch up on his sleep.

When Sukumar was a child, his grandmother called him a *vanavasi*— forest dweller—because he spent so much time exploring the woods. But it wasn't until he entered the doctoral program in ecology at the Indian Institute of Science in Bangalore that he decided to study elephants.

∧ Villagers surround a crop-raiding bull elephant that has been electrocuted by farmers.

In 1980, keenly aware of the Asian elephant's uncertain future, Sukumar immersed himself in the life of the jungle. From his forest bungalow at Hasanur, Sukumar had a beautiful view of the surrounding hills and rainforests. At night, he could hear the elephants rumbling and moving through the forest behind his house.

Sukumar identified as many elephants as he could. The bulls were easy to recognize by the shape and size of their tusks. The females proved more of a challenge, since most have only tushes. Eventually he managed to single out over 200 individuals.

< Asian elephant populations have plummeted and today they are only found in small numbers scattered across 13 countries.

Raman Sukumar measures elephant dung to estimate an elephant's age, and will collect it for genetic analysis.

To help him understand why elephants raid crops, Sukumar looked for factors that influenced their feeding in the wild. He discovered that even when there are plenty of wild grasses available, elephants prefer cultivated crops like cereals. These not only have more minerals and twice as much protein as wild grasses, but they also taste better.

Moreover, he learned that crop raids almost always happen at night, and that males join forces more often than females. Bulls are also more dangerous for farmers to confront. Why do they raid so aggressively? "To dominate in the mating game," Sukumar explains, "a bull has to be bigger and healthier than other bulls." Females, on the other hand, seem only to raid crops when they come across them by chance.

In 1986, Sukumar helped plan the 2,150-square-mile (3,500 km²) Nilgiris Biosphere Reserve in southern India, a region that's home to the largest population of Asian elephants in the world. Soon after, he began a long-term study of the elephants in the reserve's Mudumalai Sanctuary.

Today, Sukumar and his staff are using innovative means to reduce the human-elephant conflict, such as digging trenches between forests and fields and erecting electric fences, with some success. The scientists also survey villagers' attitudes toward elephants and encourage them to support conservation. And since nearly one third of Asian elephants live in captivity, Sukumar and his team are involved in putting together a health-care manual for keepers.

∧ A 7-foot ditch in Bandipur National Park, India, keeps elephants out of farmers' fields.

After more than two decades, Sukumar has witnessed firsthand the rich life cycle of elephants, from birth through mating and rearing of young, to death. "Elephants can be funny, frightening and heartwarming," he says, "and their study can be addictive." In 2003, Sukumar was awarded the prestigious Whitley Gold Award for a lifetime of work in conservation.

As for the animal's future? "If the habitat continues to shrink, the elephants will have nowhere to go. If tuskers continue to be killed at the present rate, there is a danger that there will be too few left to breed," he says. "Unless humans can achieve a balance between their own legitimate needs and the needs of their fellow creatures, there may be little hope for the elephant."

SOUNDS LIKE A HERD OF ELEPHANTS

Elephants communicate using touch, smell, and sight, but their most significant exchanges are through sound.

Grunts, rumbles, trumpets, screams, snorts, bellows, barks and purrs are just some of the sounds that make up the elephant's vast vocal repertoire. Scientists are only beginning to decipher what these mean, but they know that special calls are linked to playfulness, fright, reassurance, aggression and defense. Trumpeting announces an emergency—an animal is lost, or being threatened or attacked. (Though young elephants also trumpet in play.) The "let's go" rumble tells a family when it's time to move. Calves mumble their own "it's time to nurse" call, or announce, "I want to play." By changing the size of the long, wide nostrils running up its trunk, an elephant can modify sounds that start out in its larynx, or voice box.

Some vocalizations are made by only one sex, some by both, and others solely by babies. Because their lives are more socially complex, females have three to four times as many calls as males. They can even recognize those from groups they rarely associate with. They call in chorus with other relatives, while males do not.

< When elephants meet they lift their trunks high to convey a range of messages, from friendly greetings to warnings of aggression.

I n single file, the researchers follow a red sand path as it winds its way deep into a forest, in Dzanga-Ndoki National Park in the Central African Republic. Then the hikers wade waist-deep through a swamp until they are back on dry ground, surrounded by thick forest and singing African gray parrots. At last, the forest opens to reveal a huge thatch-roofed platform. Here, overlooking a 30-acre (12 ha) clearing known as Dzanga Bai, the researchers' journey comes to an end.

∧ Researcher Andrea Turkalo observes some of the forest elephants in her study.

Katy Payne describes the area as "the most breathtakingly ideal place for the study of elephants I could possibly imagine." She's made the journey with fellow biologists and an engineer from the Bioacoustics Research Program at Cornell University in New York. They are all part of the Elephant Listening Project (ELP), launched in 2000 to learn more about Africa's elusive forest elephants. From here the team can eavesdrop on up to 120 forest elephants that gather every day to drink and dig minerals from the soil.

Biologists estimate that as many as 300,000 individuals—half of the continent's elephants—live in the dense forests of west and central Africa. While they understand that the forest-dwelling species is gravely threatened by poaching, logging and human settlements, they know little else about these animals. And until now, researchers could estimate their numbers only by hiking through the dense bush, counting piles of elephant dung.

"The more we learn about elephants, the more we realize how much there still is to learn," Payne explains. "Our first objective is their numbers and locations, but what we learn will be richer than that. Perhaps our project will help secure the future of these animals."

Forest elephants have long been elusive to scientists. But new technology is changing that.

Andrea Turkalo, a former biology teacher who has spent 11 years documenting the behavior of the elephants at Dzanga Bai, is also part of the ELP expedition. Turkalo's long-term study of these elephants—the largest forest-elephant population in the world—is the only one of its kind. She has identified and tracked over 2,500 individuals here, and her intimate knowledge of the elephants and their relationships contributes immensely to ELP's research.

> In its first field season, the team buried tiny microphones half a yard (45 cm) deep inside termite mounds. Meanwhile, atop the observation platform, surrounded by cameras, binoculars and solar-powered computers, the researchers carefully observed the elephants below.

After three months, the team returned to New York to begin the long task of analyzing their data. So far, Payne and research assistants Mya Thompson and Melissa Groo have logged over 17,000 elephant calls. "Calls reveal something about population dynamics— the more elephants there are in one place, the more calls you get," says Groo. In other words, counting calls is a valid way to count elephants.

∧ TOP: Perched on a platform overlooking Dzanga Bai, researcher Melissa Groo gets a bird's-eye view of the daily activities of the forest elephants below.
BOTTOM: Specialized recording units capture elephants' calls at the same time that a video camera captures their behavior.

Calls may also someday be a reliable gauge of age, sex and breeding habits. The researchers have discovered that females and calves call much more than bulls, and have more overlapping calls—like people talking all at once. Eventually, they would like to build a sort of elephant dictionary, in which they record the possible meaning of certain calls.

The ELP team is also working in Kakum National Park in Ghana, where—unlike in Dzanga Bai—elephants are rarely seen. Here researchers estimate elephant numbers with both recording units and the dung-counting technique. (One unit recorded over 3,000 calls, though researchers never spotted a single elephant.) Eventually, they'll compare the two methods' findings.

Acoustic monitoring may someday be used to follow elephant migration, warn farmers about crop-raiding elephants and alert anti-poaching units when gunshots go off.

"When you eavesdrop on conversations between friends and relatives," says Payne, "you find out how they think, what is most important to them, how they adapt to new situations and so forth. Acoustic monitoring carries us forward in our relation with these animals on two fronts. The first has to do with science. The second has to do with the morality that develops as we gain understanding of what is real in the lives of others."

Biologist Katy Payne had spent 15 years listening to whale songs, so it was natural for her to wonder about the sounds other huge mammals use to communicate. On a whim, she visited Oregon's Washington Park Zoo in 1984, and spent a week listening to and watching the zoo's elephants. But it wasn't what Payne *saw* that would change the direction of her research—and her life. It was what she *felt*.

Payne noticed a faint throbbing in the air near the elephant's cage, and remembered feeling similar vibrations as a child, beside the organ in choir. Those same shudders were caused by low, barely-audible musical tones. Four months later, Payne returned to the zoo with two colleagues and some borrowed sound equipment. Together they confirmed what Payne had already guessed—elephants communicate using infrasound, sound so low that people cannot hear it.

Payne went on to study elephant communication in Kenya and Namibia, discovering that elephants hear and respond to one another's calls from distances as great as 2.5 miles (4 km). In Zimbabwe, Payne took part in a study that used radio collars to explore the remarkable way elephants use infrasound. The study found that bulls can pinpoint the whereabouts of cows ready to mate, even across great distances. Given that females are in estrus (ready to mate) for only a few days every four or five years, this is quite a feat. Infrasound also allows separated family groups to continue moving in the same direction, even when they are seemingly out of hearing range.

∧ Researcher Katy Payne pioneered studies showing elephants communicate with calls too low-pitched for humans to hear.

Currently, Payne is involved in the Elephant Listening Project and remains passionately concerned about the survival of these mysterious mammals.

SHOULD ELEPHANTS BE KEPT IN ZOOS?

A 2002 study by the UK's Royal Society for the Prevention of Cruelty to Animals (RSPCA) pointed out the problems linked with keeping such large, intelligent animals in zoos.

There is no question that captive elephants lead an unnatural life. Zoo elephants do not learn in their natural habitat, and as a result, certain behaviors will not be passed down through generations. Small enclosures can translate to bored and distressed animals. The RSPCA study found that elephants in European zoos often are unhealthy, overweight and have a shorter lifespan than their wild counterparts.

∧ Paintings by elephants help raise funds for conservation groups and zoos.

Yet many scientists argue that captive elephants have an increasingly important role to play in wild-elephant conservation. Many zoos do strive to ensure their animals' comfort and well being, and some even have the space and funds to create savanna-like landscapes. Zoos also contribute valuable research data to scientists studying wild populations. Researchers can collect information from captive elephants that couldn't be gathered in the wild—about communication, reproduction, nutritional needs and diseases.

Every year, millions of admiring zoogoers are awed by these animals. Once they learn of the difficulties facing wild elephants, people appreciate the need to protect them and conserve their habitats, and often make an effort to help.

Plus, many zoos have breeding programs that strive to maintain a healthy, diverse captive elephant population. This acts like an insurance policy: if necessary, the captive gene pool can be used to introduce new variations to wild populations.

< It's critical that elephants are housed in large enclosures that mimic their natural habitat.

Charlie Gray always knew he would spend his life working with elephants. As a youngster, he was attracted by their size and intelligence and read everything about them that he could get his hands on. Today, Gray cares for the 13 elephants that make their home at the African Lion Safari in Ontario, Canada. He's made a name for himself through his dedication to elephant conservation, breeding and management.

∧ A keeper at the African Lion Safari tends to an elephant's foot. Keepers put in long hours washing, scrubbing, feeding and exercising their charges.

The African Lion Safari had kept both African and Asian elephants since 1971, but when Gray was hired in 1985, he concentrated on the more endangered Asian species. Gray and his crew of keepers have had amazing success at breeding their initial group of 12 Asian elephants (seven females, five males). Eight baby elephants have been born at the park, and Gray has been there for every birth.

Gray attributes the program's success to the elephants' nutritious diet and frequent exercise. The animals live in a large, dynamic social group, just as they would in the wild. "By giving them a variety of daily activities, we keep the elephants healthy mentally, physically, emotionally and socially."

Working with scientists at the nearby University of Guelph, his team uses blood samples and other tests to choose the best candidates. Once a female is pregnant, her gestation—nearly two years long—is monitored by ultrasound, and her keepers ensure that she walks and swims to stay strong and fit. A couple of months before the elephant's due date, the keepers maintain a 24-hour watch on the mom-to-be.

Since 1985, Charlie Gray has been caring for the elephants at the African Lion Safari, where eight baby elephants have been born.

Gray, who lives with his wife and daughter at the African Lion Safari, puts in long hours. A typical day starts at 7:30 a.m. After the barn is cleaned, each elephant is washed and scrubbed to keep it free of dead skin, abscesses and ingrown hairs. In the afternoon, the elephants are exercised and trained, then watered and fed again at 6 p.m. Each day, an adult elephant eats 200 to 300 pounds (90 to 135 kg) of hay, 5 pounds (2 kg) of oats, and treats of fruits and vegetables. In addition, they're taken to the woods to browse on grapevines and willow, maple and apple trees. At around 10 p.m. the keeper heads back to the barn for one last round of cleaning and feeding.

Gray is not just dedicated to his family of elephants at the park, but also involved in international conservation, education and research programs. "The more we know about reproductive biology, the more easily we can apply it to wild elephants," says Gray. "I just want to make sure there are elephants around for generations to enjoy, like I have."

By the time the tiny 6-week-old elephant was found deep in a rock depression, she was clinging to life. Without her herd to take care of her, the baby, named Seraa by her rescuers, had become an orphan. Days later, a helicopter transported her to the Nairobi Elephant Nursery. As the chopper touched down, Seraa's tiny trunk waved from an open window. It will be many years before she's ready to rejoin a wild herd, but she's in good hands.

∧ Daphne Sheldrick, Africa's "elephant mother," with an orphaned elephant.

In 1977, Daphne Sheldrick founded the David Sheldrick Wildlife Trust, in memory of her husband, the founding warden of Tsavo East National Park in Kenya. The trust helps fund the orphanage at her home in Nairobi, where keepers work around the clock. Often dehydrated and sunburned, some elephants brought here were separated from their families. Others suffer from anxiety, having witnessed the slaughter of their families by poachers or angry farmers.

Renowned as Africa's "elephant mother," Sheldrick was the first person in the world to hand-rear a baby elephant, and she and her team have successfully raised some 32 newborns. Sheldrick's success is the result of almost 50 years of painstaking work perfecting a milk formula for infant elephants. Early on, however, she realized that the orphans' need for companionship was just as strong as their nutritional needs.

A 5-week-old orphaned calf playfully nuzzles its keeper at the David Sheldrick Wildlife Trust Orphanage in Kenya. Keepers must become the elephant's surrogate parents.

It's not easy being an elephant caregiver. The keepers must become the orphans' new family, and help them develop the strong sense of security they'll need when they return to the wild. Working in shifts, keepers sleep with each elephant to provide physical contact. Caregivers even dress alike so the calves will recognize them easily. They take the orphans for walks in the forest, where they might meet up with wild elephant groups. They play with them, give them mud baths and even rub their skin with coconut oil.

When a baby is roughly 2 years old, it is taken to Tsavo East National Park, where it is gradually reintroduced to the wild. Housed at night in a protective stockade, it is free to mingle with wild herds by day. By around age 10, it will live independently of humans.

Interestingly, some elephants come back to visit their keepers and other orphans. Orphan Taru, an established member of the wild community, returned for a brief visit after two years away. Lissa proudly returned in 1999 to show off her first wild-born calf. Other elephants never come back, severing all ties with humans. Either way, Sheldrick's goal has been achieved—they are wild elephants again, no longer in need of their adopted families.

WHAT IS THE ELEPHANT'S FUTURE?

"Although our generation will not witness the last of these extraordinary creatures, ours may be the generation that decides their fate," says biologist Joyce Poole. "Will we stand by and watch as the remaining elephants are killed by ivory poachers, shot for raiding crops or fenced into small protected areas to be culled on a regular basis? Or will we have the imagination and the courage to find a better way to live with elephants?"

"Ours may be the generation that decides their fate."

Some African and Asian countries have set aside nature reserves and national parks where elephants are protected from poachers. But more parks—and larger ones—are needed.

Outside protected areas, local people need to be given a reason to keep elephants alive and healthy. The animals must be seen as an asset to the community, instead of a burden. For example, money from safaris and elephant tours might compensate farmers who have lost crops, or be used to build schools, hospitals and roads.

Better law enforcement and anti-poaching patrols can help deter hunting, catch offenders and stop the international trade in illegal ivory. Some conservationists argue that ivory could be taken from elephants that die of natural causes. Others promote substitutes such as coroso, a fruit pit of the ivory palm tree that has a similar color and texture.

Scientists warn that there is not enough data on elephant numbers, distribution, habitats and behavior, and urge for more money to be spent on research.

Strong political will, sound science, hard work and creativity must work hand in hand to ensure the elephant's survival.

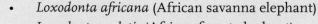

FAST FACTS

Scientific name
- *Loxodonta africana* (African savanna elephant)
- *Loxodonta cyclotis* (African forest elephant)
- *Elephas maximus* (Asian elephant, 3 subspecies)

Size
- male African elephants weigh up to 15,000 pounds (6,800 kg) and stand up to 13 feet (4 m) tall; females up to 7,125 pounds (3,200 kg) and 8.5 feet (2.6 m)
- male Asian elephants weigh up to 11,900 pounds (5,400 kg) and stand up to 10.5 feet (3.2 m) tall; females up to 9,200 pounds (4,200 kg) and 8 feet (2.4 m)
- African elephant's tallest point is the top of its shoulder, which arches higher than the head. Asian elephant's tallest point is at the top of their head

Life span
- 60 to 70 years; after humans, the longest life span of all mammals

Locomotion
- normal walking speed about 4 mph (6.5 kph); can reach 15 mph (24 kph) when being chased or charging enemies
- must always keep one foot on the ground, so cannot gallop, trot or jump
- excellent swimmer; can stay in water for six hours without touching bottom; when submerged, trunk is used like a snorkel

Trunk
- up to 300 pounds (135 kg) and 6 feet (1.8 m) long
- equipped with 150,000 muscle units, it can pluck a single berry off a tree, lift 600 pounds or tenderly stroke a family member
- used like a hose, can hold more than 2 gallons (7.5 l) of water

Feet
- elastic, spongy pad of tissue on each sole acts as a shock absorber, to support the animal and muffle noise
- African elephants have four toes on front feet, three on back; Asian elephants have five on front, four on back
- toes are buried inside the flesh, with only the nails showing

Skin	•	close to 1.5 inches (3.8 cm) thick on back and soles of feet, but paper-thin inside ears and mouth

- no sweat glands to help cool off, so must depend on mud baths
- African elephant's skin is more wrinkled and less hairy than Asian species

Teeth and Tusks

- ivory tusks are elongated incisors that continue to grow throughout life
- male and female African elephants have tusks; tusks of female Asian elephants are absent or too small to be seen
- adults have 24 molars, with large, sharp ridges to crush and grind plants
- teeth are replaced horizontally, as on a conveyor belt, with new teeth growing from the back of the jaw

Ears

- in the African elephant, can weigh up to 110 pounds (50 kg) and measure 5 feet (1.5 m) across and 6 feet (1.8 m) high—at least three times the size of an Asian elephant's ears
- African elephant ears are shaped roughly like a map of Africa; Asian elephant ears roughly like a map of India
- blood vessels in ears work like car radiators to prevent overheating
- widely spaced to trap low-frequency sound waves

Reproduction

- pregnancy lasts 18 to 22 months, the longest in the animal world
- mating can occur at any time of year, but usually during rainy season
- females are ready to mate between the ages of 10 and 18, but only come into estrus (heat) once every four or five years
- bulls enter first musth—a state of aggressive eagerness to mate— at age 25 to 30 for African elephants, age 15 to 20 for Asian elephants
- litter is almost always a single calf; up to 12 offspring in a lifetime
- calves nurse until 3 to 6 years old

HOW YOU CAN HELP

If you would like to learn more about elephants or the projects designed to protect them, contact one the following organizations:

African Elephant Conservation Trust
www.elephanttrust.org

10 State Street, Newburyport, MA, U.S.A. 01950
Phone (978) 352-2589

Born Free Foundation/Elefriends
www.bornfree.org.uk/elefriends

3 Grove House, Foundry Lane, Horsham, West Sussex RH13 5PL
United Kingdom

Conservation International
www.conservation.org

1919 M Street NW, Suite 600, Washington, DC, U.S.A. 20036
Phone (202) 912-1000

David Sheldrick Wildlife Trust
www.sheldrickwildlifetrust.org

1 Hunterfield Park, Gorebridge, Midlothian EH23 4AY, Scotland
United Kingdom

International Elephant Foundation
www.elephantconservation.org

P.O. Box 366, Azle, TX, U.S.A. 76098

Wildlife Conservation Society
wcs.org

2300 Southern Blvd., Bronx, NY, U.S.A. 10460
Phone (713) 220-5100

World Wildlife Fund Canada
www.wwfcanada.org

245 Eglinton Avenue East, Suite 410, Toronto, ON, Canada M4P 3J1
Phone (800) 26-PANDA or (416) 489-8800

World Wildlife Fund US
www.worldwildlife.org

1250 Twenty-Fourth Street NW, P.O. Box 97180,
Washington, DC, U.S.A. 20090-7180
Phone (800) CALL-WWF

Demonstrators protest the ivory trade in Kenya. The African elephant's future is at stake; only a full ban on ivory trade will save it from poachers.

For more information about elephants, visit these Web sites:

Elephant Information Repository   *elephant.elehost.com*

Elephanteria   *www.himandus.net/elephanteria*

Peace Parks Foundation   *www.peaceparks.org*

Save the Elephants   *www.save-the-elephants.org*

Savanna Elephant Vocalization Project   *www.elephantvoices.org*

INDEX

PHOTO CREDITS

AUTHOR'S NOTE

To Blair and Adrienne, whose generation will inherit not only the wildlife on the Earth, but also the ongoing task of ensuring its survival.

Sincere thanks to Melissa Groo and Raman Sukumar for reviewing the book. Thanks also to editor Dan Bortolotti for his enthusiasm and confidence in this project, to Tracy Read for her suggestions and advice, and to Clive for his never-ending support and encouragement.